IMAGES
*of England*

# KILBURN AND CRICKLEWOOD

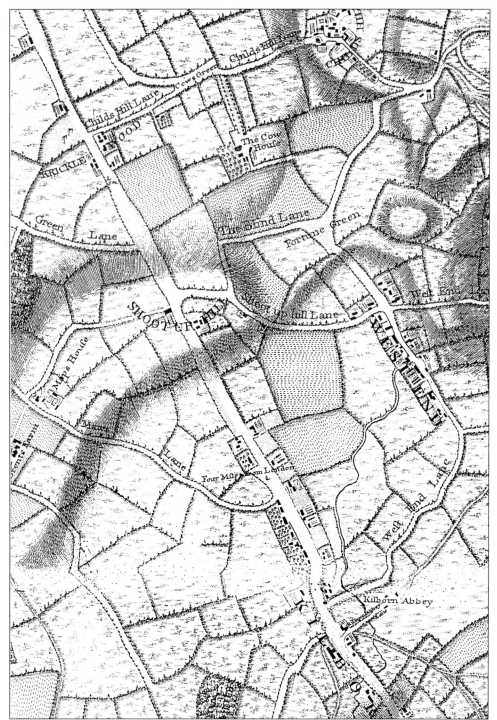

Rocque's map from around 1745, shows the Edgware Road passing through 'Kilborn' and 'Kricklewood'. The stream under West End Lane, 'Kilborn' Abbey and a line of houses along the main road in Kilburn, are clearly depicted. Cricklewood comprised a small cluster of houses near the junction with Cricklewood Lane, then called Childs Hill Lane.

IMAGES
*of England*

# KILBURN AND
# CRICKLEWOOD

*Compiled by*
Marianne Colloms and Dick Weindling

TEMPUS

First published 2001
Copyright © Marianne Colloms and Dick Weindling, 2001

Tempus Publishing Limited
The Mill, Brimscombe Port,
Stroud, Gloucestershire, GL5 2QG

ISBN 0 7524 2449 1

Typesetting and origination by
Tempus Publishing Limited
Printed in Great Britain by
Midway Colour Print, Wiltshire

A greetings card from Kilburn, posted in 1923, with two general views of Kilburn High Road and three of Grange Park.

# Contents

# Acknowledgements

The authors would like to thank the staff of Brent Local History Archive and the staff of Barnet Local History Archive for their help. Special thanks are due to the staff of the Camden Local Studies and Archives Centre for their continuing help and co-operation. Thanks are also due to James Crook and Jean Smith for allowing us to publish copies of their photographs; and to Kevin Hosey of Hendon Rifle Club for providing information.

All illustrations are copyright and reproduced with the kind permission of the following:
The London Borough of Barnet: Grape Vine Cottage p. 66, Cricklewood Tavern p. 85; The London Borough of Camden: Cover, Rocque Map p. 2, Brass p. 11, The Bell p. 12, Kilburn Mill p. 14, Brondesbury Manor House p. 20, Health Centre p. 53, Holy Trinity engraving p. 57, Gordon Memorial Schools p. 58, Oaklands p. 19, Kilburn High Road shops p. 78, Cock watercolour p. 82, Smyrna Mansions p. 29; Tom Conti: portrait p. 32; Alan Coren: portrait p. 36; Cricklewood Redevelopment Company: image p. 128; James James Crook: 3 views along Kilburn High Road pp 9, 10 and 13, Stanmore Cottage p. 22, Brondesbury Terrace p. 31, Baptist Chapel p. 42, Williams p. 73, Lord Palmerston p. 109, Gouberts p. 114; Trevor Potter, Abbey Foresters: dinner p. 47, hall p. 50; Margery Gretton: Mapesbury House p. 23; Keith Cheyney, Haberdashers' Aske's School Archive: 4 images of Westbere Road School and grounds, pp 64-65; Handley Page Association: portrait p. 117, aerodrome p. 118, hanger p. 120, royal visitors p. 121; John Lewis Partnership Archive: Spedan Lewis p. 27; Mildred Loss: Joe Loss p. 34; The Jewish Museum: Zangwill portrait p. 26; John Laing plc: Golders Green Estate p. 122; Ken Livingstone, Mayor of London: portrait p. 35; Metropolitan Police: P.C. Hunt p. 52; Powell-Cotton Museum: Henry Perry Cotton p. 22; Royal College of Music: Eric Coates p. 31, Garcia p. 33; Jean Smith: Palmerston Baths p. 48, ARPs p. 51, Stamps p. 67, Quex Mews p. 72, Kilburn Wells playbill p. 98, Broadway cinema p. 99, Kingsgate Street party p. 100, Crooks 1860 p. 114; Richard Bayliss, The Smiths Group: aerial photo p. 125, bridge p. 126, headquarters p. 126, royal visit p. 126, van p. 126; Fred Taylor: two Bentley cars p. 124; Thomas Estates Ltd: Beacon Club p. 103.

All other illustrations are from the personal archives of Marianne Colloms and Dick Weindling. The authors have made every effort to trace the owners of each image.

# Introduction

Today's Edgware Road follows the line of Watling Street which was built by the Romans soon after they landed in AD 43. It provided a means of rapidly transporting troops from their fort at Richborough, Kent, to London and north to Chester. Kilburn and Cricklewood began as small villages on both sides of the busy road. The early public houses offered a range of services from stabling to food, accommodation and entertainment. Some are still in business today. At Kilburn, the Edgware Road formed the boundary between the Hampstead and Willesden parishes. Cricklewood was divided between Willesden, Hampstead and Hendon parishes. Today the modern boroughs of Camden, Brent, Barnet and Westminster cover these areas.

In the early nineteenth century the farmland was mainly used for fodder or to graze livestock. In particular, the care and rearing of horses made an important contribution to the Willesden economy. Kilburn and Cricklewood were country neighbourhoods, around a hour's horse ride from Marble Arch. They attracted a number of very wealthy residents, 'the gentry', who built or took over existing large houses. In 1829 the area was still rural enough for a local resident to describe a stag hunt. The animal got as far as Kilburn Priory before turning towards Paddington, where it was cornered inside the parish church!

Suburban development began in south Kilburn in the mid-nineteenth century and spread slowly north along both sides of the Kilburn High Road and Edgware Road. Developments were mainly aimed at the growing middle and more prosperous working classes. Those with more money headed for the leafy avenues of Brondesbury and some of the streets off Shoot Up Hill. By the turn of the century, many of the south Kilburn streets where building had begun in the 1850s were already showing signs of decline. Properties were generally subdivided into flats or rooms. This was also true of the area around Palmerston Road. Following the Second World, both Hampstead and Willesden Councils began a programme of clearances and renewals in Kilburn.

As building spread, so new churches were built to meet the needs of a growing population. Faiths other than Church of England began to establish themselves in the expanding suburbs. Attendances generally declined after the Second World War, forcing the closure of a number of older places of worship, some of which were adapted for use by new communities, notably to serve Hindu and Islamic worshippers. Others have disappeared altogether, to be replaced by new, secular buildings.

Before there were any compulsory laws, education was a hit and miss affair. If you had money, you could hire a home tutor or send your child to a private school; otherwise, many children started work as soon as they could. The churches started a programme of school building while state education dates from 1870.

During the nineteenth century the growth of retailing in Kilburn and Cricklewood provided many jobs; large shops such as the Bon Marche also had live-in-staff. Other major employers were on the Willesden side of the main road, such as Saxby and Farmer's signal works and the Kilburn Brewery. Although both districts were cut through by rail lines, the Midland Railway alone provided a significant number of jobs at its Cricklewood depot. The rural character of Brondesbury and more particularly Cricklewood, that persisted up until the First World War, sustained nursery gardens and stables. The outbreak of war gave a great boost to industry, notably the production of aeroplanes, and led to the creation of Cricklewood Aerodrome. At one point in a small group of streets off Edgware Road, there were no less than three aeroplane companies. Industry diversified after the war and the entire north Cricklewood area, along the Edgware Road and up to the North Circular Road, became a major light industrial area. In 1931, over 6,000 people worked in factories here and by 1937 Willesden was officially the largest manufacturing borough in the entire country! Recent years have seen a significant downturn in manufacturing industry with many of the older Cricklewood companies closing or moving away, among them Smith's Industries and Rolls Razors. Today superstores on trading estates are probably the largest local employers.

Kilburn had a few small shops by the early nineteenth century; Cricklewood was more remote and had almost none. In addition to several pubs and beer houses, 1829 Kilburn already had nineteen traders, among them George Ball, 'perfumer and hair cutter.' Here early shops were created from existing houses or cottages by either taking over the ground floor, or in the late nineteenth century, building over a front garden. Street traders were a common sight. The years leading up to the First World War saw both Kilburn and Cricklewood established as major shopping centres. As described by a local resident: 'The High Road delighted me. The shops were all kept by individualists and each one seemed to have its own character. The multiple store was almost unknown, the only exception to the best of my recollection being Sainsbury's.' Shop windows were used to display as many goods as possible and residents were loyal to a certain butcher or baker, so several could exist within quite a short distance. Major changes came after the Second World War with the progressive expansion of self-service stores and multiples or chain stores.

Today, traffic congestion is a major problem for the main road through Kilburn and Cricklewood. However, Edgware Road has always carried traffic, from Roman troops, to experimental steam engines, horse buses and trams. Public transport during the nineteenth century made it possible for families to move further from their place of work. However, it took a long time for fares to become affordable by all but the better paid. And until the bicycle came along, personal transport was largely the preserve of the wealthy or the traders, in some sort of horse-drawn vehicle.

Since the Second World War the population has become more diverse. Irish, African-Caribbean and more recently Asian communities have become established in Kilburn and Cricklewood.

# One

# Early Days

This early photograph probably dates from the 1860s. Taken by James Crook, the Kilburn undertaker, it looks south down the High Road. On the left are some small shops, later the site of B.B. Evans' department store. The large building in the middle of the picture is 'Leith House' situated on the corner of today's Quex Road.

Crook took a series of photographs moving north along Kilburn High Road. The tall building was Muncey's dairy. Charles Muncey started as a cowkeeper in Kilburn in the 1840s, and by the 1860s was running the dairy. The dirt road is virtually deserted.

This small brass tablet is thought to represent Emma de Sancto Omero, prioress of Kilburn around 1400. The earliest known building in Kilburn, the priory was established as a small Benedictine nunnery in 1134, near today's Belsize Road and Kilburn Vale. The brass is the only remaining physical evidence of the priory and is kept in Saint Mary's church, Abbey Road.

This building is all that was left of Kilburn Priory around 1750. For 400 years the nuns provided food and shelter for travellers and pilgrims to St Albans. It had several buildings including a church, a house, a brewery and bakehouse. After the Dissolution of the monasteries in 1536, the priory became a private house and a farm, until the remains were pulled down in 1790.

During the eighteenth century people came to Kilburn Wells to drink the curative water from a spring in the grounds of the Bell Tavern. The well was near the corner of the High Road and today's Belsize Road. The grounds were also used for music and dancing, duelling and bare-knuckle fighting. The Bell remained popular as a tea garden after the popularity of 'taking the waters' declined.

THE GUARDS PRACTISING AT THE VICTORIA RIFLE-GROUND, KILBURN.

The Victoria Rifles practicing at their Kilburn range in 1855. The 'Cumberland Sharpshooters' were formed in 1792 and moved to a new range in Kilburn in 1849. The club became a military unit in 1853 known as the 'Victoria Rifles' and Queen Victoria and the Duke of Wellington would come to review the troops. They left Kilburn in 1867 when Victoria Road was built.

A strange Victorian story concerned the 'bleeding stone of Kilburn'. Sir Walter Scott, pictured here, wrote a poem which told of the medieval murder of Sir Gervase de Merton in Whitby, by his brother Stephen, for the love of Sir Gervase's wife. Gervase bled to death on a stone which Stephen later brought to Kilburn, as a shrine to his brother. He confessed to the murder when blood gushed from the stone. In fact, the story was invented by Scott and his architect friend William Atkinson. Atkinson had used some stones from the remains of Kilburn Priory in his St Johns Wood garden, and around 1817 he added a large stone with an iron-red stain which he had shipped from Whitby.

Another early photograph by James Crook looking across the High Road over Muncey's dairy, towards Abbey Road in the distance. Behind the shops the old bridge over the Kilbourne stream which ran alongside the High Road can just be seen. Today there is no sign of the stream as it was put into a culvert and covered over in the 1860s.

THE AUTHOR OF "WAVERLEY."

According to local tradition, Oliver Goldsmith wrote *The Vicar of Wakefield* while staying in Kilburn in the 1760s. There's no proof of this, but the possibility cannot be ruled out, as he was constantly moving from place to place to avoid creditors. His name was remembered by a small street at the bottom end of Kilburn called 'Goldsmith Place' (now Springfield Lane).

Around 1798 a windmill was built on the top of Shoot Up Hill. The origin of this name is uncertain, but may refer to its steep slope. On 23 December 1863 a gale blew the windmill's sails around so fast that friction caused a fire, which destroyed most of the windmill. An eye-witness said: 'I thought it was a beautiful sight to see it going round and round in flames, like a Catherine wheel'. The remains of the windmill were finally removed around 1905.

# Two

# Rural Scenes

CRICKLEWOOD          OLD COTTAGES     OXGATE LANE, 2

These cottages stood in today's Oxgate Lane. 'Oxgate' supposedly refers to the Saxon word 'oxgang' meaning the area an ox could plough in one year, around 15 acres. In 1902 the area was described as 'among the prettiest in the parish, with its luxuriant hedgerows, in which many varieties of wild flowers grow.' The cottages were demolished in 1937.

Westcroft Farm, Cricklewood Lane, was 'The Home of Rest for Horses' from 1909 until the mid-1930s. The Home was opened by its president, the Duke of Portland, and was briefly famous in the 1920s when American cowboy filmstar, Tom Mix, kept his horses there.

A horse could be transported to and from the Home in a specially designed 'Horse Ambulance.' During the First World War, the Home sent a fully equipped ambulance to help the many thousands of horses that served on the French Front.

CLOCK HOUSE FARM.

Clock House Farm on Edgware Road, roughly opposite Cricklewood Lane, took its name from the clock in its barn gable. The farmer bought the doors and the clock from the demolished Tyburn tollgate near the present Marble Arch, and built both into his barn. The barn was demolished in 1892.

*Avenue Farm Cricklewood N.W.*

Avenue Farm off Cricklewood Lane. Sent in 1909, the message on the card reads: 'Uncle may remember this road as the one he used to go to fetch the milk'. The last tenants were the Dickers family. The 'Misses Dickers' lived in the farmhouse and kept much of the land as fields, until it was finally developed in the 1930s.

17

This nineteenth-century engraving by 'SP', identity unknown, was thought to be Mill Lane, looking towards the tower of Hampstead parish church. But the low bridge almost certainly places it on West End Lane, a short distance from the Kilburn High Road. Here the Lane crossed the Kilbourne, one of several local streams.

# *Three*
# Men of Property

The house in the background is Oaklands, on West End Lane between today's Cotleigh and Dynham roads. Charles Asprey, the Bond Street jeweller lived there in the 1850s. Sir Charles Murray bought the house in 1872. While in Egypt as the Consul General, he arranged for the first hippopotamus to be shipped back to the London Zoo. When Murray left, the estate was sold for building in 1883.

W.H. Smith Jnrx, of the newspaper shop empire, became an MP and in 1877 was made First Lord of the Admiralty. In 1839 his father bought 'Kilburn House', which stood near today's Priory Park Road. At four in the morning, father and son would travel to their head office in the Strand. The family stayed in Kilburn until 1856 when building development forced them out to Hertfordshire.

Brondesbury Manor House on Willesden Lane was mentioned as early as 1246. Lady Sarah Salusbury owned the property in 1789 when Humphry Repton, the great landscape gardener, laid out the grounds. In 1821 it was occupied by Sir Coutts Trotter, a member of the great banking family. Leased as a school from 1882 until 1934, it was demolished to make way for Manor House Drive.

This red brick mansion, The Grange, stood close to Kilburn High Road in grounds which stretched as far as Kingsgate Road. The last owner was Ada Britannia Peters, widow of a successful coachbuilder. Following her death in 1910, the contents of the house were sold in an auction that lasted three days. The house was demolished and the grounds became Grange Park.

In 1831 William Harrison Ainsworth began to write a novel about Dick Turpin called *Rookwood*. While living at The Elms (where the Kilburn State is today) Ainsworth used descriptions of Kilburn as background for the book. To get material for Turpin's famous ride to York, Ainsworth, who was a good horseman, said he performed the ride himself to show that it was possible.

Kilburn Lodge and Stanmore Lodge stood roughly where Nos 290-300 Kilburn High Road are today. This picture was taken in the early 1880s, on the day of an auction sale prior to demolition. Even the windows were for sale, marked as lots 35 and 46.

Henry Powell Cotton was a major property owner in Kilburn and Cricklewood, with some 160 acres reaching almost to the Crown pub. Following the death of his wife after an unhappy marriage, Henry married his mistress Charlotte. The couple lived for many years in Kingsgate Lodge, a large house on Shoot Up Hill.

References to Mapesbury House on Willesden Lane date from 1519. When a new kitchen was being fitted in 1897 a cast iron chimney was discovered with the date of 1594 embossed on it. In the mid-nineteenth century the house was used as horse training centre. Edmund Yates wrote his best-selling novel *Broken to Harness* while staying at the house in 1863. It continued to be used for horse training until 1916 and was pulled down in 1925.

Pictured in the 1890s, Cricklewood Lodge at the corner of Walm Lane was the estate office for All Souls College, Oxford. The college owned land at Kensal Green, Willesden and Cricklewood. Chichele Road is named after the college founder and Anson Road after the Warden. The Lodge is currently a hotel.

Cricklewood House stood next door to the Crown, at the corner of Cricklewood Lane. William Roper who founded the Kilburn 'Bon Marche' store lived here with his wife in the 1880s and 90s. Celebrations for their silver wedding anniversary included a garden marquee, with enough space for a ballroom and dining area. The house was demolished around 1900.

The Revd Huntington lived at 'Cricklewood House' from 1798 to 1811. After a succession of jobs including gunmaker's apprentice, hearse-driver, gardener and coal heaver, he had a vision of Christ and became a preacher. He used the title 'S.S.' to signify 'sinner saved' and continued to call himself a coal heaver. Huntington managed to raise £10,000 to build a chapel in Gray's Inn Lane and worked there until his death in Tunbridge Wells in 1813.

# *Four*
# Home Sweet Home

Cambridge Road was a densely populated, mainly working class neighbourhood. The Edwardian photograph looks towards the junction with Granville Road. Much of the area was demolished as part of mass clearances and redevelopment of the district after the Second World War. Note the boy on the unusual bicycle.

Posted in 1907, this card shows the end of Cambridge Avenue with Kilburn High Road in the distance. In 1949, Willesden Council recorded population densities of between 180 and 150 persons an acre, compared with 30 for Brondesbury Park. Much of the neighbourhood was redeveloped but the houses on the right survived. Several are now listed.

Israel Zangwill, the 'Jewish Dickens', around 1891 when he used the pseudonym 'Marshallik', which means 'fool'. He lived at No. 24 Oxford Road from 1893 to 1899, and was a member of the 'Wanderers of Kilburn', a group of Jewish intellectuals who lived locally. They met in each other's homes to discuss literary and cultural issues. In 1895 Theodor Herzl visited Zangwill at Oxford Road, and modern Zionism was created.

John Spedan Lewis pictured in the 1930s, created the John Lewis Partnership. He lived in North Hall, a large house in Mortimer Crescent. Lewis helped establish Whipsnade Zoo and had an aviary at North Hall, under the care of a Mr Gander! He also kept a lynx in a cage at the end of the tennis court. The family moved in the 1930s.

Carlton Vale and its junction with Canterbury Road, between the wars. The large Saxby and Farmer factory was in Canterbury Road and the shop on the right sells workmens' overalls. The iron railings in the middle of the road mark the site of a largely vanished institution, the public lavatory. Most of the neighbourhood was swept away by post Second World War clearances.

Looking west along Christchurch Avenue towards Willesden Lane. The sender of this card, posted on 5 May 1913, at 1.15 p.m. in Kilburn, was confident it would arrive in time to cancel a date with a friend in Hornsey that evening! The piles by the side of the road are not in fact the by-product of horses, but the neat efforts of the local road sweeper!

THE INGLE NOOK.

This was the 1904 Christmas card sent by Mr and Mrs Lillie Mitchell of Ingle Nook, No. 181 Walm Lane. Victorian householders often commissioned a photograph of their house, with themselves standing proudly on the doorstep. The resulting card could be adapted to cover a variety of occasions. The family stayed until the end of the First World War.

An architect's drawing of Smyrna Mansions, built in 1898. At the end of the nineteenth century, the idea of living in a purpose-built flat gained popularity. Some blocks included servants' quarters, while Smyrna Mansions was supplied with electricity, still a rarity. However, the tenant of a top floor flat near Kilburn Tube wrote to a friend: 'fancy 100 stairs to climb every time!'

Play!
Where is the ball coming?

This cartoon was drawn by Louis Wain who lived at No. 41 Brondesbury Road from 1916. He pictured cats in all sorts of human situations: fashionably dressed, at parties or playing games. Hugely popular, it was said that Christmas without a Wain was like a pudding with no currants! Sadly Wain was diagnosed as suffering from schizophrenia in 1924 and spent the rest of his life in mental institutions. He continued painting but his cats grew increasingly abstract and brightly coloured.

The original large houses and St Paul's church in Kilburn Square were demolished in 1964, when a shopping precinct and the seventeen-storey block of flats were built. In 1993 part of the area was opened as a market for a range of small traders selling discount goods.

An early picture of Kilburn High Road, probably dating from the 1860s. It looks north, at the elegant Brondesbury Terrace, now the site of the Kilburn State. The small figure is standing at the entrance to 'The Terrace', a road that still exists and originally led to a row of houses.

In 1906 the composer Eric Coates lived over a shop on Kilburn High Road. He travelled 'on top of a rickety old horse-bus, bumping uncomfortably over the cobbles', to study at the Royal Academy of Music. In 1913 he moved to a house near the junction of Abbey and Quex Roads. Called 'the uncrowned king of light music', Coates' best known composition is probably the 'The Dam Busters' March (1955).

During the 1970s and 1980s, Tom Conti lived in Exeter Road and Mowbray Road. He originally trained as a classical pianist but changed to acting. Conti gained critical acclaim for his stage performance in *Whose Life Is It Anyway?* where he played a paralysed sculptor. He is best known to cinema audiences for *Shirley Valentine* (1989) and *Merry Christmas, Mr Lawrence*, (1983).

Looking down Exeter Road towards Walm Lane, the large house on the corner with St Gabriels Road is being decorated. The iron railings that front the houses on the right were a typical feature of Victorian streets. Many were removed during the Second World War and have never been replaced. The elegantly dressed women reflect the middle class nature of this area.

Shoot Up Hill looking north beyond Kilburn Underground station, was lined with a series of villas by the end of the nineteenth century. The horse bus slowly climbing the hill on its way to Cricklewood, ran to Charing Cross via Marble Arch.

Senor Manuel Garcia lived at 'Mon Abri', No. 27 Shoot Up Hill, from around 1879 until 1906. Garcia was a famous singing teacher who invented the 'laryngoscope'. This allowed examination of the larynx and helped diagnose disease. He followed a simple lifestyle: 'rarely does he take more than a roll or a glass of milk for lunch: he never smokes: and takes but little wine.' Perhaps this contributed to his longevity, as Garcia died aged 101!

The virtuoso violinist, Max Jaffa lived at three addresses in Cricklewood – No. 2 Ivy Road, Hillcrest Court on Shoot Up Hill and Ashton Court off the Broadway. His neighbours in Hillcrest Court were the young sisters, and later stars, Joan and Jackie Collins. Jaffa won the Gold Medal at Guildhall School of Music and got his big break in 1929 with weekly BBC radio broadcasts. His 'Palm Court' style was very popular with TV audiences. Max did a season at Scarborough in 1960 and repeated this for the next twenty-seven years.

The famous bandleader, Joe Loss, moved to No. 16 Kendall Court on Shoot Up Hill in the 1930s. His good friend Max Jaffa lived nearby. The Joe Loss band was extremely popular and toured extensively. Their record of *Begin the Beguine* was a hit in 1939 and has sold over a million copies. Joe was awarded a fifty-year contract with EMI and frequently played at Buckingham Palace and Windsor. He died in 1990, but the 'Joe Loss Orchestra' is still performing.

Mrs Blanche Conyers Morrell, a talented artist and illustrator, is pictured in the garden of No. 22 St Gabriels Road, around 1906. The house belonged to her sister Henrietta Daubney.

Ken Livingstone, the MP for Brent East since 1987, has lived in several addresses in the area, including Gascony Avenue and Kingsgate Road. He worked as a technician before qualifying as a teacher. Livingstone was a councillor for Lambeth and Camden and became leader of the Greater London Council in 1981. He is currently the first elected Mayor of London.

Alan Coren, journalist and broadcaster, lived for many years in Ranulf Road and put Cricklewood on the map through a series of humorous articles and books. Alan joined the staff of *Punch* in 1963 and became editor in 1977. He moved to *The Listener* but in 1987 decided to work as a freelance writer and broadcaster. A long serving panellist on Radio 4's *The News Quiz* and BBC's *Call my Bluff*, he has recently moved out of the area.

# *Five*
# Spiritual Matters

The Wesleyan church in Quex Road with its large classical portico by J. Tarring, opened in 1869. It could seat 900, but the congregation had fallen to just 200 by 1961, when the church faced a £20,000 estimate for roof repairs! The site was redeveloped as a block of flats with a smaller, two-storey church in Kingsgate Road.

St John's, Oxford Road, was built in 1871 with seating for 1,000 worshippers; the architects were F. and F.J. Francis. St John's closed in its centenary year and following a disastrous fire in 1975, the building was demolished. Note the ornamental pair of stone eagles on the gate pillars to the left.

St James Congregational chapel in Cambridge Avenue was open by 1872. An unlikely survivor, the prefabricated metal building was a temporary structure, intended to be replaced by brick. The chapel had ceased to function by 1902; subsequently it became Cambridge Hall and is currently used by Sea Cadets. It is Grade 2 listed.

The original St Paul's, Kilburn Square, was the oldest place of worship in Kilburn, and opened in the 1820s. Enlarged in the 1880s and 1890s, the church was noted for its music under Henry Bonavia Hunt, founder of the Trinity College of Music, London. St Paul's closed in 1936 and was finally demolished in the 1960s.

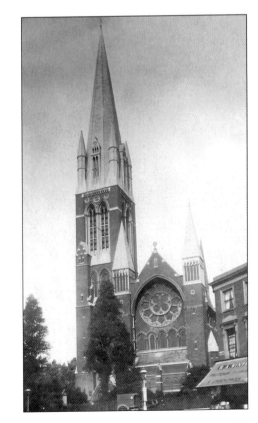

One of London's largest Victorian churches, John Loughborough Pearson designed St Augustine's, considered to be his best work. Consecrated in 1880, the church was finally completed eighteen years later with the addition of a 254ft high spire, the tallest in London. The acoustics are particularly good and the building is much used for recording sessions.

The Boys' Brigade, from St Mary's church, Abbey Road, at their 1911 summer camp in Whitstable. Glasgow Sunday School teacher William Smith started the Brigade in 1883. He developed 'drill and discipline', combining games and sport with hymns and prayers. A simple uniform was introduced, consisting of a 'pill box' forage cap, a haversack with a broad white strap and leather belt.

In 1866 the Oblates of St Mary Immaculate purchased land for a church in Quex Road. Edward Welby Pugin was the architect and the Sacred Heart Roman Catholic church opened in 1879. A 150 ft spire was planned but never built. During the 1960s more than 10,000 worshippers attended the eighteen masses celebrated every Sunday, figures which exceeded attendance at most cathedrals!

Built in 1888, St George's Presbyterian church stood on the corner of Willesden Lane and Deerhurst Road. It clearly looked older than it was; the Belgian visitor who sent this card in 1902 described it as a *tres ancien monument!* St George's closed in 1973 and the site has been redeveloped as the Shree Swaminarayan Temple.

The Shree Swaminarayan Hindu Temple, Willesden Lane opened in 1988. In 1975, Temple members bought the disused St George's church (above) but needed more space. In 1986 the church and adjoining building were demolished to build the temple. It is a substantial and attractive brick building with colourful, traditional Indian decoration whose roof is topped by two small domes and a spire.

The ornate Brondesbury Baptist chapel on the corner of Iverson Road, soon after its completion in 1878, before the Metropolitan Railway Bridge was built across the High Road the following year. In 1902 the services were described as 'bright and helpful, the worship devout'. It closed in 1980 and was demolished, to be replaced by a block of flats.

Opened in June 1900, the leasehold site for the Presbyterian church in Rondu Road cost £9,000. In 1957, two years after permission was refused for the conversion of the church into a television studio, the site was compulsorily purchased by Hampstead Council and used for a block of flats.

The three children posing rather awkwardly in their Sunday best are standing outside the first St Michael's church, opened in 1907 and later used as the parish hall. It is now a French school. Three years later, the present church was built alongside, at the corner of Mora Road.

Children from St Luke's, Fernhead Road, which opened in 1877. The vicar remembered 'green fields surrounded the church south and west; our summer Sunday worship was often disturbed by the bleating of sheep, who wandered up to the very church doors.' The beautifully dressed girls carry cards, spelling out the name of the Revd G.E. Higgins, vicar of St Luke's from 1914 to 1935.

The Salvation Army opened barracks in Percy Road, Kilburn, in 1889. Both photographs are of the 'Kilburn number 1' band. The man seated immediately behind the drum in the top photograph features again in the lower picture (dated 1919) as the conductor carrying a baton. The Salvation Army recognised the value of music in promoting the gospel. Popular tunes were adapted: *Way down upon the Swanee River* became 'Joy, freedom, peace and ceaseless blessing'!

This Gothic-style Congregational chapel in Chichele Road was designed by Walter Wallis and completed in 1902. It has an orange terracotta façade. By 1978 the congregation had fallen to just twenty-one, and the chapel was closed. It reopened as a mosque and Islamic center two years later. Currently the building is being renovated.

St Gabriel's Walm Lane was consecrated in 1897. A lightening strike caused some £1,000 worth of damage to the roof in July 1900 but it was repaired and the church completed in 1902-1903. This included the distinctive 'saddleback' tower. The church is Grade 2 listed.

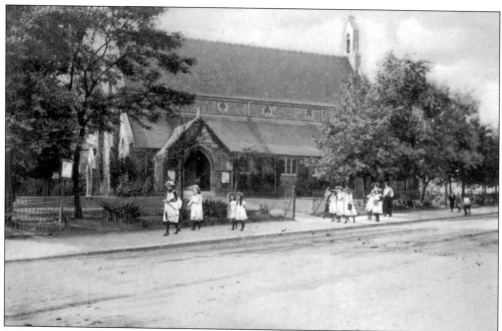

St Peter's, Cricklewood Lane, was consecrated in 1892. Employees from the nearby Handley Page factory made regular use of the church hall for social events, talks and even boxing matches! In the 1970s St Peter's was demolished and replaced by a smaller church which finally closed in 1983. Today the site is a carpark, but the hall remains.

A large number of Jewish residents moved to Brondesbury and Willesden Green in the late nineteenth century. Brondesbury Synagogue in Chevening Road opened in 1905. Damaged by fire in 1966, it subsequently closed and as shown today, forms part of the Al-Khoei Foundation.

# Six

# Civic Duty

A dinner in the hall of the Ancient Order of Foresters, soon after the Kilburn High Road building opened in 1928. During the Second World War the premises were used to dispense orange juice and cod liver oil to local children. The property was returned to the Foresters who kept the front shop as an office, but sold the large hall to Brent Council in 1951. It became the Tricycle Theatre in the 1980.

Opened in June 1886, the Palmerston Road baths provided washing facilities for people who had no bathrooms. A cold bath was a penny while a warm bath cost twopence. The baths were closed in 1976. During demolition, they were damaged by a massive gas explosion which blew out 200 windows on the nearby Webheath estate.

The Kilburn, Willesden and St Johns Wood volunteer fire brigade was established in 1863 following the fire that destroyed the windmill on Shoot Up Hill. In 1894 a new fire station was opened in Salusbury Road which covered the Kilburn area until the Seond World War. Kilburn Public Library, on the right, was also opened in 1894 and enlarged in 1908.

The RSPCA moved into No. 10 Cambridge Avenue in March 1931. When the dispensary was formally opened a year later it had already treated over 6,000 animals. The premises consisted of a surgery and waiting room, kennels and a glass-fronted cattery. The dispensary continues to help sick animals today.

This large bronze appears on the front of the RSPCA building. Since the 1920s there had been calls for a war memorial to animals who served in the First World War. However, it was not until the early 1930s when the RSPCA, assisted by the Royal Society of British Sculptors, promoted a competition for the memorial design. The winner was F. Brook Hitch of Hertford.

In 1845 the 'Abbey Foresters' court, or branch of the Foresters, was formed. They took the name because one of the founders owned the Abbey Tavern in St John's Wood, where the group met for the next thirty-seven years. As a benevolent society they helped members with sickness payments and mortgages. In 1924 they purchased a cottage at No. 269 Kilburn High Road, and erected the building shown here, shortly after completion in 1928.

Grange Park opened to the public in 1913. The Grange house and estate off the High Road was put up for sale in 1910. A 'Kilburn Open Space' appeal only managed to raise £600. Finally in 1911, Hampstead and Willesden Councils stepped in and bought the property for £19,500 (including the money from the appeal). At today's prices this is over a million pounds.

These Kilburn Air Raid Precaution wardens (ARPs for short) were photographed during the Second World War, outside Smyrna Mansions. The warden service was part of Civil Defence. They reported details of air raids and were trained in first aid, in order to provide help until the rescue services arrived.

PC Hunt served at West Hampstead police station from 1903 to 1928. 'S' Division covered the eastern side of the Kilburn High Road. After the end of the First World War thirty-five men were dismissed from 'S' Division for their part in a strike which won the right for an eight-hour day for their colleagues.

The Willesden Local Board offices were opened in 1891 in Dyne Road. This was the administrative centre for Willesden until 1972 when the office moved to Brent Town Hall at Wembley. The Dyne Road building was then demolished and replaced by a block of flats called 'James Stewart House', in memory of the first chairman of the Board who had a shop in Kilburn High Road.

Mrs Lucy Baldwin opened the Health Centre in Kingsgate Road in 1929. Her husband, Stanley Baldwin, was Prime Minister three times. He successfully steered Britain through the general strike and the abdication of Edward VIII. The building is presently the Kingsgate Community Centre, established in 1982 by a group of local people in what was then a derelict building.

Pictured in 2001, Cotleigh Road Library was constructed in 1901. It was the first purpose-built library in Hampstead, replacing a temporary one at No. 48 Priory Road. It had a newsroom, a magazine room and wood-block floors 'for quietness'. Recently threatened with closure or the removal of the book-lending service, a local pressure group has campaigned to keep it open.

The chapels of Paddington Cemetery, opened in 1855. Paddington was one of three cemeteries sold off by Westminster Council; in 1984, Brent Council bought it for just £1. Arthur Orton, the claimant in the famous Tichborne trial is buried here, in an unmarked grave. In 1854 Sir Roger Tichborne was presumed drowned at sea but his mother refused to believe Roger was dead. Ten years later a man answering his description appeared in Australia, working as a butcher. He came to England to claim his inheritance. But after two lengthy trials, Arthur Orton, who was born in Wapping, was found guilty of perjury and served ten years in jail. Reduced to making appearances in Kilburn pubs for a few pennies, Orton died in poverty in 1898. The case achieved such notoriety that 5,000 people attended the funeral and the name 'Sir Roger Tichborne' was engraved on the coffin. A film was made of the story in 1998 and a book has recently been published, claiming Orton really was Sir Roger.

# Seven
# Education and Health

This photograph of a class at Kingsgate School, Messina Avenue, was taken on Empire Day, 1928. The day chosen for this patriotic celebration of the British Empire was 24 May, the birthday of Queen Victoria. In the 1930s Gerry Anderson, who later created *Thunderbirds* and other TV series, was a pupil at Kingsgate Infants school.

Number 36 Quex Road was St Leonard's girls' school from 1903 until 1907. Private schools were a feature of Victorian Kilburn but like St Leonards, many were short lived. The house has been demolished and its site now forms part of the new St Mary's Primary School.

St Peter's Home, Mortimer Road was open by 1871. Run by the St Peter's Sisterhood, 'for respectable sick persons', women and young children were accepted, but not chronic invalids, or 'patients suffering from cancer, mental diseases, fits, imbecility, ringworm, or diseases caused by intemperance.' The Home closed in the 1940s.

This engraving of Holy Trinity School, opened in 1847, dates from the 1860s. The school stood next to the Victoria Rifle ground, close to the Cock public house on Kilburn High Road.

This 1920s photograph shows a bleak, cramped room. A scribbled note on the back says 'Kilburn, our class' but the location is unknown. The pupils, all girls, are clean but poorly dressed. The blackboard notes show they were studying the *Domesday Book*.

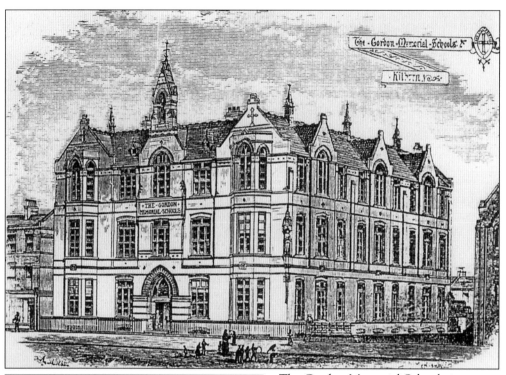

The Gordon Memorial Schools in Cambridge Road, opened in 1887, for 1,240 boys, girls and infants. One of three schools promoted by local fundraiser Emily Ayekbourn, its name commemorated General Gordon, killed at the siege of Khartoum in 1885. The school closed in 1953 when the buildings were bought by St Mary's Roman Catholic School. It has since been demolished.

Built in 1870, St Mary's School stood on West End Lane near the Kilburn High Road. In 1991, the pupils moved from this small, restricted site to a modern building at the corner of Quex Road. The old school is currently in use as a nursery.

There were two schools in Kilburn Lane. The clothing worn by the boys in this Edwardian photograph indicates it was a class in the board school at the Chamberlayne Road end of the Lane, opened in 1885.

The Salisbury Road Primary School opened in 1902, for 1,260 pupils. After 1944 it became a secondary modern but this department closed in 1970 and the school reverted to its original primary status. This picture, taken in the early part of the twentieth century, shows pupils and staff assembled in the main hall.

Brondesbury Military Hospital in Brondesbury Park, was founded by Miss Maude Thomas, Commandant of the St John's Ambulance Association Voluntary Aid Detachment. During the First World War, many large properties were taken over as nursing homes. The hospital was established in 'Beversbrook', a large detached house donated by Dr Vaughan.

A group of First World War convalescent soldiers pose for their picture on the garden steps of 'Beversbrook'. Note the wickerwork wheel chair on the right. The house became a general nursing home after the war.

*St. Monica's Home Hospital, 16, Brondesbury Park, N. W. 6. North Front.*

Open by 1890, St Monica's Home Hospital for Sick Children was at No. 16 Brondesbury Park. In 1939, its president was the Duke of Devonshire. The hospital then had 26 beds and annual running costs of £2,300 which were about double the assured income. It became a geriatric hospital which closed in 1976 and was demolished in 1980.

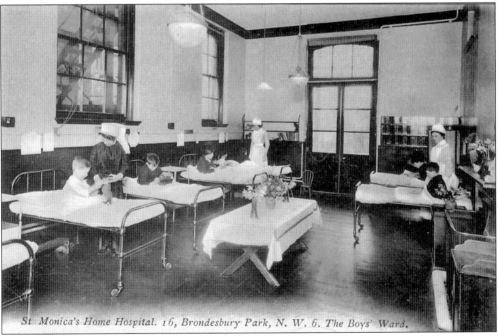

*St. Monica's Home Hospital. 16, Brondesbury Park, N. W. 6. The Boys' Ward.*

Presumably this postcard and others of the hospital were printed and sold to raise funds. Here the boys and staff have been carefully posed, each child shown holding a toy or book, in a perfectly-made bed.

61

The Maria Grey Teacher Training College opened in 1892 on the corner of Salusbury and Chevening Roads. It shared the building with the private Brondesbury and Kilburn High School. Today the building is part of the Al-Khoei Foundation and houses an Islamic school.

A class in the Maria Grey College. When it first opened the College was on the edge of the open countryside. A student in the college magazine wrote: 'we walked through wide hayfields and larks sang to us.'

This building in Priory Park Road dates from the mid-1930s, when Willesden Polytechnic was reorganized as Kilburn Polytechnic. It is now part of the College of North West London. An interesting ex-student is the current King of the Asantes, Otumfuo Osei TuTu II, who studied human resource development at Kilburn Polyetchnic.

Girls in the tailoring class at Kilburn Polytechnic, in the 1930s. They learnt needlework and tailoring, with time set aside to continue their general education.

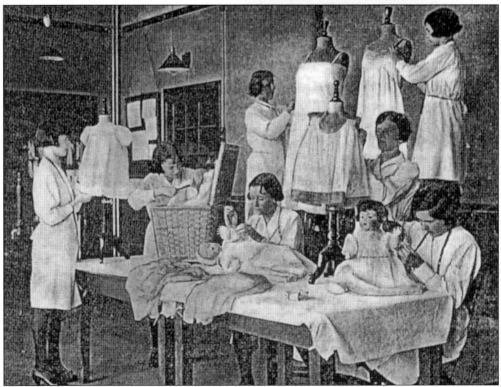

In 1898 the old Haberdashers' Company School (founded in 1690) decided to build a new school, away from Hoxton. In 1899 the school moved into temporary accommodation in two houses on Cricklewood Broadway, north of Cricklewood Lane. In 1901 a site was purchased in Westbere Road, where the new school opened two years later.

An assembly at Haberdashers' Aske's school, which opened in 1903. By 1911 there were 503 pupils. Annual fees in 1913 were £15 for boys aged eight to nineteen years, and half of this for juniors aged five to eight years.

A cricket match at Haberdashers', probably shortly before the First World War.

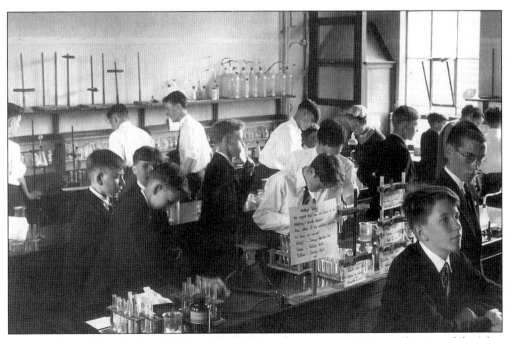

An open day at the school, probably in the 1950s, and parents are visiting a chemistry lab. After almost sixty years, in July 1961 Haberdashers' Aske's moved to Elstree and Hampstead School took over the Westbere Road site.

Grape Vine Cottage originally stood near Finchley Road. It was the 'dame school' for Childs Hill village, but as the numbers of pupils increased, more space was needed. So the cottage was mounted on rollers and moved down the hill to a larger site alongside the Cricklewood Tavern in Cricklewood Lane. A plot of land was fenced off and a second school room added. Infant classes were taught at Grape Vine Cottage until 1870, when they moved into the nearby National School. Despite much protest, the cottage was finally demolished in 1981.

# *Eight*
# The Kilburn Traders

These two shops in Queens Terrace on Kilburn High Road, were north of West End Lane. In 1880 Charles Stamp took over a cheesemongers (hence the 'established 1825' sign). The window of his wife's shop, 'The Kilburn Bonnet Box', is filled with a dense display of hats. Stamp traded until the mid-1890s when he sold on his business.

Looking south down Kilburn High Road from its junction with Belsize Road around 1909, towards the 'Bon Marche', a large draper's shop. At the time, it was promoting a new range of corsets: 'guaranteed absolutely rustless; one will be displayed in a tank of water, thus conclusively proving they will not induce rust stains upon the wearer's underclothing.'

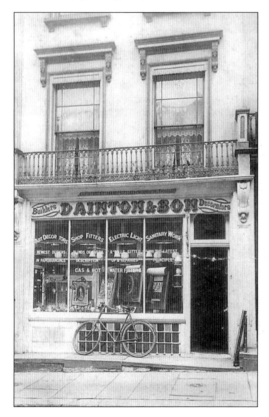

Dainton and Son at No. 234 Belsize Road. Samuel Joseph Dainton was one of the many builders who helped create Victorian Kilburn and made enough money to buy a comfortable house in St Johns Wood. This card was posted by an employee at 1.15 p.m. on 19 June 1906, to let his family know he'd be late home that same night!

The banner across the High Road reads 'you cannot better Kilburn'. A special 'Shops Week' was held in May 1909. The promoters' claim that Kilburn could satisfy 'the most exacting requirements' was borne out by the variety and quality of goods on sale. Some 300 shops along the High Road offered items as diverse as food, clothes, bicycles, books, jewellery, home furnishings and musical instruments.

Posted in 1907, by a French visitor who called it *la grande rue due quartier de Kilburn*. Parrs Bank and Philips music shop stood on opposite corners of West End Lane; Philips moved here in 1891. He hired pianos for 10s a month, 'kept in tune free'. The shop closed in the 1930s but the medallions of composers' heads still decorate the first storey.

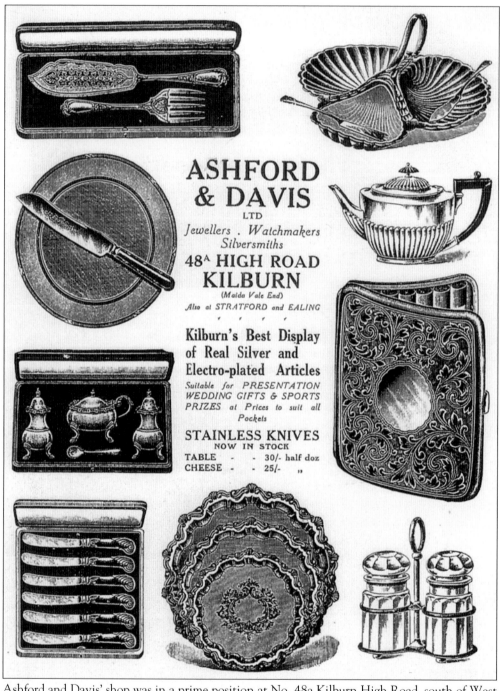

**ASHFORD & DAVIS**

LTD

*Jewellers . Watchmakers Silversmiths*

**48ᴬ HIGH ROAD KILBURN**

(Maida Vale End)

*Also at STRATFORD and EALING*

**Kilburn's Best Display of Real Silver and Electro-plated Articles**

*Suitable for PRESENTATION WEDDING GIFTS & SPORTS PRIZES at Prices to suit all Pockets*

**STAINLESS KNIVES**

NOW IN STOCK

TABLE - - 30/- half doz
CHEESE - - 25/- ,,

Ashford and Davis' shop was in a prime position at No. 48a Kilburn High Road, south of West End Lane. Opened by 1894, this advertisement dates from 1919. The shop became part of the Samuels' chain after 1945.

Opened in 1897 by Benjamin Beardmore Evans, his shop grew from a single premise to occupy Nos 142-162 Kilburn High Road. It became the district's premier department store. The cluttered displays were typical of the time; during the shops' promotions week in May 1909, B.B.Evans ran a competition to select its best-dressed windows. This card shows the shop in the early 1900s.

On 13 January 1910, a fire gutted the shop. None of the staff who lived over the premises were hurt but most lost their possessions. B.B.Evans was rebuilt and expanded to forty separate departments. It finally closed in 1971 after a last massive sale.

Stabling in Quex Mews was first occupied by the Crook family in 1878. Four of their horses were much admired when they pulled the Kilburn Volunteer Fire Brigade engine in the 1881 Lord Mayor's Show. The Crook family are listed as Kilburn residents from 1854 and worked from various addresses as carpenters, builders, jobmasters (hiring carriages and horses) and undertakers.

In 1880 Crook's the undertakers opened at No. 259 Kilburn High Road, on the corner with Buckley Road. Previously 'Crook's Kilburn Economical Funeral Establishment' was at Clarence Place, opposite today's Kilburn State. Many of the earliest photographs of Kilburn were taken by James Crook and until recently the undertakers was run by James' descendants. Several family members are buried in nearby Paddington Cemetery.

In the 1870s Thomas Williams moved to a cottage in Clarence Place (later No. 256 Kilburn High Road). The writer Thomas Hardy found lodgings nearby during his brief stay in Kilburn in 1862-1863. This picture was taken after 1894, when Alfred Williams took over the business which sold fishing rods (a faded sign over the door says 'The Golden Carp, established 1850') as well as making and repairing umbrellas. It closed in 1922.

Kilburn High Road, looking south from Willesden Lane in the early 1920s. A bicycle and rider cross the junction in a blur of speed. But a local landmark is missing on the right, the tall tower of the State Cinema, which replaced a run of shops in 1937.

This view from the corner of Willesden Lane was taken soon after 1907, when two motorized bus services ran along Kilburn High Road. Fosters the wine merchants offered their customers a wide range of beverages, from champagne to whiskey, bottled beer to tea. The Domestic Agency which opened in 1896 in rooms above Fosters, had servants for hire.

Boons & Sons were at No. 81 Willesden Lane, just off the Kilburn High Road. One window is full of sweets in bottles, the other, cigarettes. The picture can be precisely dated to Friday 1 October 1915 from the *Daily News*, declaring: '121 guns captured in Champagne'. There is also an advert for a film at the Kilburn Empire, starring Walter Passmore and Florence Wray.

Customers of Pegrams, No. 222 Kilburn High Road, could take advantage of a 'profits sharing club'. Bovril was an 1870s invention. The company claimed it did you good and encouraged other foods to give up more of their nourishing qualities! The name came from 'Bo' (Latin for ox) and 'vril', a name for 'life force' coined in a contemporary novel.

In the late 1880s Simon Abraham Marks took over a greengrocers shop at No. 302 Kilburn High Road. Note the three gas lamps to illuminate the display and the wooden pediment over a cashier's cabin. It was common to pay at a desk inside the shop, rather than give cash to the assistant. The shop traded under the name S.A. Marks until the 1940s.

An early branch of J. Sainsbury's, showing their extensive Christmas display of 1907 at Nos 292-294 Kilburn High Road. This was their Brondesbury 'high class' shop, opened in 1888. The walls were decorated with coloured tiles depicting a floral vine and birds eating fruit. Today the building houses a community project.

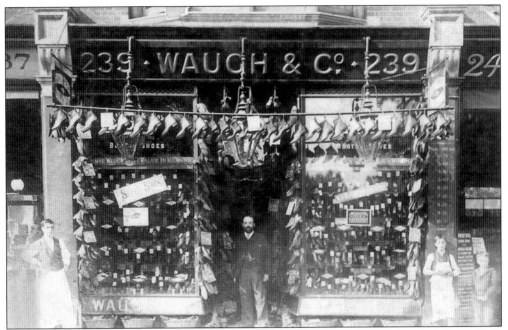

The smiling Mr Waugh opened (and closed) his boot and shoe shop at No. 239 Kilburn High Road in the 1890s. At No. 321, another shoe shop was reputedly haunted by a poltergeist. The workbench was smashed and tools and left hand shoes were thrown about. After three weeks, the disturbances ceased as suddenly as they had begun.

This photograph taken in the early years of the twentieth century, looks north up Kilburn High Road, towards the Brondesbury Baptist Chapel on the corner of Iverson Road. The row of cabs on the left served Brondesbury station.

A short stretch of the Kilburn High Road in the 1880s, north of the Black Lion pub, where Nos 276-282 stand today. The shops are in the converted ground floors of what had been private houses; Normans Dining Rooms were then offering a good dinner for 6d, steak puddings at 4d and tea or a teacake 2d. In 1884, they were one of the outlets selling tickets for the Temperance fête (see p. 103).

# Nine
# Time Gentlemen Please!

The Queens Arms first appears in an 1845 directory. The tavern had pleasure gardens which sloped down to the Kilbourne stream. This picture was taken during the 1890s when the London General Omnibus Company had a depot for their horse buses in the pub yard. The present Queens Arms is a modern building.

Another of the very old Kilburn pubs photographed in 2001. The Red Lion was probably established in the seventeenth century, even though a stone set into the building claims it dates from 1444. A painting of the Red Lion by George Moreland is in the Tate. The present building was completed in 1890.

The Brondesbury Arms at the corner of Canterbury and Chichester Roads, post 1908. In 1949, Willesden Council noted there was one pub per 424 residents in this South Kilburn neighbourhood, compared with a borough wide average of one to every 4,500 persons! The pub survives today as The Bronze, but is currently derelict.

The Prince of Wales pub, shown here in 2001, appeared in a directory for 1874 as No. 11 Cambridge Gardens. Today it is a Grade 2 listed building.

Sir Colin Campbell was a distinguished soldier who fought in the Crimea and India. Campbell was knighted in 1849 and created Baron Clyde in 1858. The 'Sir Colin Campbell' pub at No. 264 Kilburn High Road, dates from the late 1850s. In the 1840s, there was a beerhouse just three doors away, with the intriguing name of 'Help the Lame Dog over the Stile'!

The Cock is one of the oldest pubs in Kilburn. It can be traced to 1723 although a plaque on today's building says it was licensed in 1486. This anonymous watercolour shows the nineteenth century building. The proprietor of The Cock from 1834 to 1838 was Henry Cribb, the brother of Tom Cribb, who had been a great prizefighter.

.THE COCK "KILBURN DISTILLERY.

The Cock burnt down and was rebuilt around 1794. This photograph shows the building after it was remodelled in 1900. A 1909 advertisement for the Kilburn Distillery at 'Ye Olde Kilburn Wine House' promoted wines from the wood, pure malt and pot still whiskies.

The Black Lion is one of the older pubs in Kilburn, dating back to the seventeenth century. Rebuilt in 1898, the ornate new building was typical of public houses of the time, and is now listed. The postcard has a note on the back: 'this is Milly's place'. Presumably she was a barmaid, living over the premises.

The Lord Palmerston, pictured in the late nineteenth century, was built in 1865. It was the terminus for horse bus services from London for many years. Surviving the clearance of adjacent Victorian property in the late 1960s and 1970s, the pub was refurbished and renamed 'The Roman Way' as Kilburn High Road follows the line of Roman Watling Street. The building is currently a restaurant.

The 'Crown' appears in 1751 licensing records. The photograph shows the nineteenth century pleasure grounds on the right-hand side. Victorian writer G.A. Sala who stayed in Cricklewood in the 1830s, recalled the potman at the 'Crown' was a Negro with a wooden leg. The man had been a cymbal player in one of the regiments at the battle of Waterloo.

The original smaller 'Crown' was rebuilt about 1898 to form today's huge Cricklewood landmark. This photograph was taken about 1904 when Henry Arthur Jones's play *Joseph Entangled* at the Haymarket was advertised on the side of the bus.

The Cricklewood Tavern at No. 75, Cricklewood Lane (or as it is called today 'The Tavern in Cricklewood'), has survived with few alterations. It still retains much of its attractive external ground floor tile ornamentation as shown in this late nineteenth century photograph.

By 1920 Magistrates had received eight applications to sell liquor from a proposed 'house' on the corner of Mora Road and Cricklewood Broadway. Although the local vicar and some residents opposed the idea, the 'Cricklewood Hotel' opened two years later. Owned by the Cannon Brewery, this explains the three profiled cannons still visible on the roof line.

The most famous owner of the Canterbury Arms was 'Jolly Jumbo', William Thomas Ecclestone, pictured here after 1908. The message written on the card reads 'Said to be a very jolly fellow, thus the reason for his nickname. He gives the neighbouring children a treat once a year and takes them all to the seaside. His wife is a very small woman.' William joined the Army as a young man, where he introduced exercises so effective they became part of standard training. He became a renowned trainer of runners and boxers in the Stonebridge area where for many years he was landlord of the Coach and Horses. His size obviously caused some problems – worried about visiting the Franco-British Exhibition he remarked sadly, 'How about the turnstiles!' Likewise, on his visits to renew his publican's license he found it impossible to pass along the narrow passages of the court house, so was allowed to sit outside in his specially made pony and trap. At the end in 1915, it took ten men to carry his coffin, while his grave was the deepest and widest ever dug in the cemetery.

*Ten*

# The Cricklewood Traders

**T. P. TIPPELL,**

**STATIONER,**

**47, CRICKLEWOOD BROADWAY.**

**DIE STAMPING.    PRINTING.    BOOKBINDING.**

**WEDDING & MOURNING CARDS.**

**DISH AND DESSERT PAPERS.    TABLE DECORATIONS.**

19
HIGHEST
AWARDS.

*Stephens' Inks*

ALWAYS
FLUID
AND
RELIABLE.

In 1909, Tippell's took over a stationer's business at No. 47 Cricklewood Broadway. Their advert shows the wide range of services they offered. Originally mourning cards were supplied by undertakers. They would give details of the name and age of the deceased person, and possibly include a text or verse, or the date and place of the funeral. The shop closed in the early 1930s.

This looks south to Shoot Up Hill. Imperial Parade dates from 1900 and marks the start of commercial Cricklewood. Continuous numbering was impractical until all buildings along a road were completed. So groups were named in 'terraces' or 'parades' to give them an identity and location. These shops were renumbered as Nos 2-22 Cricklewood Broadway by 1906. They have since been extended forward at ground level across the wide pavement.

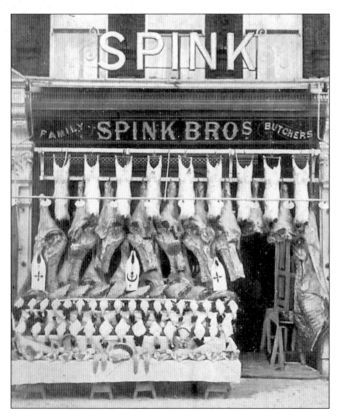

Opened at No. 23 The Parade in the 1890s, Spink's advertising card shows the unrefrigerated meat display so common at the time. Posted in 1912, the message reads 'this is a portrait of the shop I am working at, taken about five years ago, when I was junior book keeper here.' Spink had left by 1927 but the shop remained a butchers.

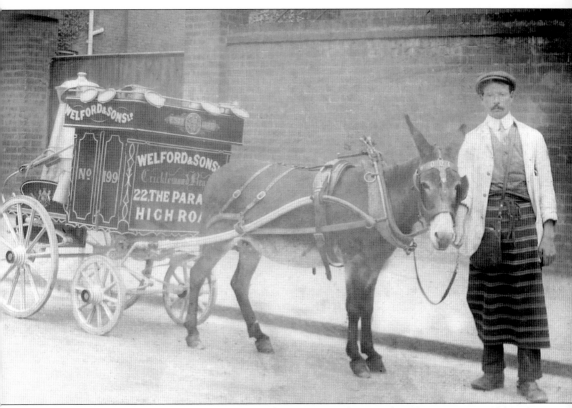

Welford & Sons Dairy was next door to Spink at No. 22 The Parade. The cart pictured here was photographed shortly before 1906, when the shop was renumbered as No. 68 Cricklewood Broadway. There was an increase in dairying outside the Metropolitan boundary following an 1864 Act which made it illegal to keep cattle in London. Welford's emerged as one of the most important dairy farmers. In the 1880s, they owned over 300 acres in Willesden and a model dairy farm at Kensal Green. This cart with its milk churns was light enough to be pulled by a donkey; her name is spelt out in brass letters on the harness: DOT. Welford's were appointed dairymen to Queen Victoria in 1876, hence the crest on the side of the cart. During the 1920s the firm was bought out by United Dairies.

In July 1912 a large crowd gathered at the junction of Anson Road and the Broadway, to unveil the 'Coronation clock'. Made of steel and wrought iron with four illuminated dials, it was a gift to the Council from local resident, Dr Ackworth, who lived on Shoot Up Hill. Subsequently neglected, it became rusty and dangerous, and was removed for salvage in 1943.

Henry Vooght's bakery at No. 110 Cricklewood Broadway was trading in 1891. By 1904, George Vooght was running the shop. As well as selling bread and cakes, Vooght's offered a pot of tea plus roll and butter for 5d. The shop changed hands during the First World War.

This looks north up the Broadway from the Windmill Hotel and public house. The card was posted in 1916 and the photograph was taken after the Coronation clock was put up at the end of Anson Road. Note the traction engine pulling a cart and the smartly dressed Edwardian mother and her children.

This postcard of shops south of the Windmill Pub was printed by Mussett's, a local stationer (see p. 94). It's probable that the photograph was taken soon after the shops were completed about 1906, as the extreme left hand premise had yet to be finished and carried an advertisement for shop leases. These shops were originally called 'Carlton Terrace'.

Highfield Model Laundry was based in Stonebridge Park. A branch was opened at No. 167 Cricklewood Broadway in 1908 and were provided with a 'residential manageress for the convenience of customers'. This picture of a proud mum and squeaky-clean child not only advertised the laundry's skills but was also calculated to appeal to most families. The shop closed in 1934.

Parke's Drug Stores at No. 67 Cricklewood Broadway opened in 1906. Hundreds of items were displayed in the window, including the ubiquitous (for the time) advertisement for rupture trusses. The message reads: 'Write or telephone. We will promptly send a messenger to fetch your prescription, your orders for any chemist goods that you may require, and deliver them without delay.'

In the 1890s John James Waghorn, bookseller, began trading at No. 14 Anson Parade. This photograph was taken before 1906, when the shop was renumbered as No. 87 Cricklewood Broadway. Waghorn's also ran a lending library costing 2s 6d a quarter to join. The shop kept its name but was sold on; by 1940 the business also offered theatre and coach bookings.

Walter Carrington had two shops on Cricklewood Broadway. In the 1890s he opened Anson House pictured on the left, (later No. 81 The Broadway). An advertisement described it as carrying 'an immense stock of corsets including "Meys Watch Spring" and "Platinum Anti-Corset" '. On the right is No. 85, where Carrington took over a drapers' business in 1906. Both shops had closed by 1916.

This long parade runs between Anson and Chichele Roads. H.E. Randall 'high class boot makers' opened in 1909 at No. 115 The Broadway. The owner of Mussett's at No. 109 stands in the doorway of his shop which sold stationery, fancy good, papers and toys. But who was the young man almost completely hidden behind the lamp-post?

Cricklewood Broadway, after 1906, when trams began running along Chichele Road on the left. By 1911, 'High Class Artificial Teeth' were available from a dentist working above the shops. This card was sent by an employee in a local firm, 'Made a start in joiners shop. Very comfortable work and nice fellows. We are singing practically all day long.'

The neighbourhood's largest draper's shop, William B. Hull, stood on the corner of Cricklewood Lane and The Broadway. Opened in 1903, it sold material and clothing. Hulls closed in the mid-1930s and was replaced by a Burton's Tailors shop in 1936. Until recently a painted sign on Cricklewood Lane advertised 'Burton's Four Guinea suit'.

Looking east from The Broadway, the tram has stopped in Cricklewood Lane. This photograph was taken after the service to Childs Hill began running in 1909. The shop on the left, Philp & Co, (everything for the home from beds to blinds) opened the same year. On the right are the windows of W. B. Hull.

# W. B. HULL

## CRICKLEWOOD BROADWAY, N.W.

## *Special Offer this Month.*

40 Pieces 35-in. PURE HEAVY CALICO at 8¾d. yard.

THIS CLOTH COULD NOT BE REPLACED UNDER 1 0. YARD.

30 Pieces, Fast Dye, Heavy Striped and Plain, NURSES' COSTUME CLOTH at 1/0¾ yard.

TO-DAY'S REGULAR PRICE 1 11½ SUITABLE FOR OVERALLS, &c.

## Special Number for this Issue.

**DAINTY VOILE BLOUSE,** Trimmed Valenciennes Lace Insertion and Embroidered Panel Fronts, V Neck.

Price - - **6/11**

**SMART LUSTRE SPORTS COAT.** Shades Stocked :—Sky, Vieu Rose, Champagne, Covert, Navy, Black.

Price - - **29/11**

This advertisement for W.B. Hull appeared in 1919 and illustrates fashionable ladies' clothing of the day, such as a 'dainty voile blouse'. Note the range of colour shades for the sports coat.

*Eleven*

# Leisure

The Maida Vale Picture Palace opened in 1913. Silent films were accompanied by a seven-piece orchestra, and in 1927 a Wurlitzer organ was installed, so powerful that the neighbours complained about the noise. The cinema closed in 1940; it became a dance hall, then a bingo club. Pictured in 2001, it is now the 'Islamic Centre England – London', opened in 1998.

# New Theatre, Kilburn Wells.

## First Night of Mr. & Mrs. SMITH's Engagement.

### On Monday Evening, the 26th of February, 1821,

Will be Performed the Tragedy of

# BERTRAM:

## Or, the Castle of St. Aldobrand.

St. Aldobrand, Mr. MATHER. Bertram, Mr. SMITH. (From the Theatre Royal, Norwich.)
Prior of St. Anselma, Mr. DOMVILLE. 1st Monk, Mr. W. MOORE.
2d Monk, Mr. HARDY. 3d Monk, Mr. WHITELEY.
Robbers, Messrs. HOWARD, MAX, & WINN.
Page, Miss POWELL. Imogine, Mrs. SMITH. (From the Theatre Royal, Norwich.)
Clotilda, Mrs. ASHTON. Child, Miss ASH.

After which a Ballet Dance, called

# THE SAILORS' RETURN:

## Or, Love in a Bustle.

Ben Backstay, with a Hornpipe, Miss POWELL. Old Gawkey, Mr. MATHER.
Jacob Gawkey, with a Comic Dance, Mr W. MOORE. Looby, Mr. DOMVILLE.
Old Woman, Mr. Moss. Miss Gawkey, Mrs. DOMVILLE. Amietta, Mrs. SMITH.

In the course of the Evening,

A Song by a *Gentleman.* A favorite Air by *Mrs. Ashton.*
A Comic Song by *Mr. W. Moore.*
A favorite Song by a *Gentleman.* (First Time.)

The whole to Conclude with the Laughable Farce of The

# BEE HIVE:

## Or, Lots of Fun.

Captain Merton, Mr. SMITH. Captain Rattan, Mr. MATHER. Joey, Mr. WHITELEY.
Mingle, with Comic Songs, Mr. G. WATSON. (His First Appearance.)
Emily, Miss POWELL. Cicely, Mrs. DOMVILLE. Mrs. Mingle, Mrs. ASHTON.

On *Wednesday Evening,* a favourite Opera and Entertainments.
On *Friday,* a celebrated Play and Musical Farce.

Tickets and Bills to be had of Mr. WHITELEY, at the Theatre, and for the accommodation
of Parties at Hampstead, of Mr. CHARLES COX, Musician.
Doors open at 6 and begin at 7 o'Clock precisely.
The Roads well watched and lighted.

Boxes 3s. Pit 2s. Gall. 1s. Second Price at half-past Eight, Boxes 2s. Pit 1s.
(NICKSON, Printer, Park Street.)

This playbill of 1821 is the earliest notice we have about entertainment in Kilburn. It promotes the visit of Mr and Mrs Smith from The Theatre Royal, Norwich. Nothing else is known about a theatre at the Kilburn Wells, which adjoined the Bell public house.

This building opened in 1906 as the Kilburn Empire music hall. Great stars such as Marie Lloyd and the escapologist Houdini played there. In 1949 it became the Essoldo Cinema, then the Classic and finally the Broadway, as seen here, which survived until 1981. The building was demolished in 1994 and the Marriott Hotel now occupies the site.

The Grange opened in 1914 as one of the largest cinemas in the country. It closed in 1975 and a year later became Butty's Nightclub and then the National Club, hosting numerous Irish show bands. In the 1980s the Sex Pistols and The Smiths performed there. The building was listed in 1991 and is currently used the Victory Christian Centre.

In the 1930s you could see the unusual Mr Jackman and his Mouse Circus in the streets of Kilburn. He previously worked as a circus clown, and then a piano-tuner. As he often caught mice inside the pianos he decided to train them, and had travelled the country with his circus since 1920. When he needed new 'performers' he visited his sister in Tunbridge Wells who kept his stock of 400 mice.

A street party in Kingsgate Road to celebrate the end of the war in 1945. These were held all over the country, with residents decorating their streets and bringing out their tables and chairs. The Kilburn children seem to have large name labels and are feasting on jam tarts and sandwiches.

The State, a Kilburn landmark with its 120ft high tower, opened in December 1937, when it was the largest cinema in Europe. The opulent decorations included black marble pillars, pink mirrors, and a candelabra which was a replica of one in Buckingham Palace. There was a very large stage and a magnificent Wurlitzer organ which still survives today. The opening programme featured Gracie Fields, George Formby and Larry Adler. During the rock and roll period, major bands played there. Jerry Lee Lewis, having married his fourteen-year-old cousin, was booed off-stage in 1958. The same year, Buddy Holly and the Crickets performed to a sell-out audience. The Rolling Stones played in 1963 and the Beatles twice, in 1963 and 1964. The State closed as a cinema in 1990, and now the listed building is only used for Bingo.

Established in 1980, the Tricycle Theatre was later severely damaged by fire but reopened in 1989. In 1998 a cinema was added, currently the only active cinema in Kilburn. Many Tricycle theatre productions have transferred to the West End and Broadway. *The Colour of Justice* (1999) was a reconstruction of the Stephen Lawrence Inquiry and was shown on BBC Television.

Situated in Cricklewood Lane, just off the Broadway, the Queen's cinema opened in 1921 on land that had previously been railway sidings. It later became a Gaumont and was demolished in 1960. The film showing when this photograph was taken in 1932 was 'The Love Contract', starring Owen Nares, a leading matinee idol.

This newly opened the Beacon Bingo Club has a large 50,000sq ft hall with 2,700 seats. Two thousand people regularly attend and annual admissions are over 600,000. Each week the individual prize is between £1,000-5,000 and so far the largest win was £215,000. The total prize money for a year is over £9 million.

This advertisement comes from a temperance magazine of 1884, when many Christian groups were attempting to counteract the 'demon drink' and persuade people to sign 'the pledge'. Several coffee houses were opened, including that of the Kilburn Temperance Council at No. 23 Canterbury Road. By organizing lots of entertainments they hoped to attract people to their cause.

## Bank Holiday, Aug. 4.

There will be a great

# TEMPERANCE ✢ FETE,

n a large field at the

### Hendon and Finchley Cross Roads, Child's Hill,

GATE OPEN 12—9.

GREAT

# BAND COMPETITION

for Drum and Fife Bands,

### ATHLETIC SPORTS,

## SWINGS, DONKEYS, COCOA-NUTS

# FIREWORKS.

There will be a

### Leg of Mutton on a Greasy Pole

to be climbed for.

### PUNCH AND JUDY. PLOTOPAHLEA.

### The Rosslyn Hill Brass Band and 12 Drum and Fife Bands.

Tea will be provided by a Committee of Ladies.—Price 8d. Adults, 6d. Children. Other Refreshments at moderate prices.

### ADMISSION 3d., CHILDREN 2d.

TICKETS can be obtained from Mr. L. R. Foot, Secretary to the Kilburn Temperance Council, at the C.E.T.S. Coffee Tavern, 23, Canterbury Road ; Mr. Box, Stationer, Promenade, High Road, Kilburn ; Norman's Coffee & Dining Rooms, High Road, Kilburn ; and from all Members of the Council

This is the dance hall and skating rink at No. 200 Cricklewood Broadway. The rink opened in 1910 and was bought by Charles Clore in 1927 who opened the Cricklewood Dance Hall alongside. Clore, who came from a poor family, became a great financier who owned most of the English shoe companies and Selfridges department store. The Cricklewood venture marked the beginning of his subsequent fortune. In 1957 the dance hall opened as the 'Galtymore', named after a mountain in Tipperary. The 'Galty' still plays Irish Country music and regularly hosts the top Irish bands.

The proud Cricklewood roller skating team of 1921-1922 posing with their championship cup. A writer went to the rink in 1937: 'For the first time in my life I have been roller skating and – if you'll pardon the vulgar Americanism – it's the cat's pyjamas'. He paid 6d entry and 2d to rent his skates but promptly fell over in the beginners' area!

This 1884 flyer advertises the Midland Railway's Bank Holiday service to the countryside just beyond Kilburn and Cricklewood. The Welsh Harp reservoir was a popular destination, due to the many attractions offered by the Old Welsh Harp pub, such as fishing, sailing, rowing, shooting, swimming, skittles, bowls and billiards. Its popularity declined with the spread of housing nearby and the Welsh Harp station closed in 1903. The pub stood near the Staples Corner flyover.

# HENDON AND CRICKLEWOOD RIFLE CLUB.

## At the NORMAL POWDER COMPANY'S RANGE,

### Renter's Lane, Hendon, N.W.

Under the Patronage
of
H.R.H. PRINCE CHRISTIAN, K.G.
Field=Marshal The EARL ROBERTS, V.C.,
K.G., K.P., P.C., G.C.B., G.C.S.I., G.C.I.E., O.M

Lord Roberts says :—" *If every English man and boy were taught to shoot, the question of the efficiency of our land forces would be solved for ever.*"

PRESENTED AS A CHALLENGE TROPHY
TO
HENDON & CRICKLEWOOD RIFLE CLUB
BY THE PRESIDENT
GUSTAF ROOS, ESQ.

The rifle club, opened by Roberts in 1906, was in Renter's Lane, (today's Claremont Road). A career soldièr, Earl Roberts was awarded the VC in 1858. When the First World War began he became commander-in-chief of the British army and left for France. Sadly he caught a chill and died in St Omer in November 1914. A very popular man and a public hero, he was buried in St Paul's Cathedral. Roberts was particularly interested in training and improving the shooting of the infantry and artillery. The Hendon Rifle club still exists at Cool Oak Lane, near the Welsh Harp.

# Twelve

# On the Move

The proud driver and conductor of a London General Omnibus Company's motor bus, serving route 1, Tower Bridge to Kilburn Station. This 'B type' was first produced in 1910. A local resident recalled his excitement: 'I remember letting all the horse buses pass so I could register my first ride on this latest invention.'

Kilburn tollgate was removed in 1864. It stood in the High Road, near the Queens Arms pub. The clock says 6.40 p.m. but there's no traffic. The gate keeper stands by his booth, which displays the rates paid by vehicles to pass through; in 1819 it cost 2s for a six-horse coach.

Kilburn Park underground station, Cambridge Avenue, in 2001. Opened in 1915, the building is clad in dark red glazed blocks and is Grade 2 listed. Its architect Leslie William Green, designed fifty stations in five years! The first 'Passimeter' was installed here in 1921, a free-standing booth with turnstiles, allowing clerks to sell and collect tickets.

The first railway passed through Kilburn in 1838 *en route* for Euston but a station was only opened in 1852, with the entrance in Belsize Road. This entrance on the High Road was added in 1879. Originally called 'Kilburn and Maida Vale', this station was renamed 'Kilburn High Road' in 1922 and is still operational.

For many years, the Lord Palmerston pub was the last stop for the Kilburn horse bus. In 1879 the fare was 5d to Charing Cross and 6d to Fenchurch Street. In the early 1900s, the service ran to the Crown, Cricklewood on Sundays, but a third horse had to be harnessed to climb Shoot Up Hill.

In addition to being a busy centre for all sorts of commercial traffic, the Crown Pub on Cricklewood Broadway was the next bus terminus up the road from the Lord Palmerston. Posted in 1907, the card shows London General Omnibus Company's open top buses, heavily covered with advertising, *en route* for Charing Cross.

*I am having a high time at Cricklewood.*

Civilian flights from Cricklewood Aerodrome began after the end of the First World War. In November 1918, 40 passengers were taken for a half hour flight and a year later, over 800 passengers were given 'joy rides' during the Easter holidays.

From the 1870s onwards, the Midland Railway built a large depot for goods and coal traffic at Cricklewood. This shows a turntable used for manoeuvring steam engines. The yards still provided over 1,300 jobs in 1949 but much of the area has since been redeveloped.

The Midland Railway opened Childs Hill and Cricklewood Station in 1870 at the corner of Cricklewood Lane and Claremont Road. When the tramline to Finchley Road was opened, the road had to be lowered in order to get tramcars under the railway bridge. Now called 'Cricklewood', some of the original station buildings are still in use.

While the Hampstead authorities refused permission for trams along Edgware Road, Willesden agreed to several lines. In 1904, eight trams an hour began running north to Edgware, from the Borough boundary near the Crown. The fare was 3d. In 1936 Willesden's trams were replaced by trolleybuses.

A Metropolitan Electric Tramways car, destination Edgware, at the Cricklewood terminus. When a tram overturned outside No. 211 The Broadway, the shopkeeper recalled the car 'was propped up by means of vinegar barrels borrowed from my shop, to release the trapped passengers.'

112

# Thirteen
# The Working Day

This 1891 wrapper advertised Samuel Clarke's Pyramid Night Lights. In the late 1870s Clarke opened a factory in a field off Cricklewood Lane. It was the first business in the area to offer jobs that were neither farm or service based. A long lived concern, it exported goods worldwide. A council estate covers the site today.

This nursery and florists at No. 2 Kilburn High Road was one of several owned locally by Jean Baptiste Goubert. This photograph was taken after his death in 1894 and the sign shows the premises as 'sold'. The site was cleared around 1899 but the Goubert family continued to trade from one of the new shops that were built.

Taken in 1860, this is one of the earliest views of Kilburn High Road to have survived. Charles Crook hired horse and carriages from this yard behind Clarence Place, a row of cottages opposite the present Kilburn State.

In 1856 John Saxby patented a signal linked to the railway points, thus dramatically reducing the chances of an accident. Going into partnership with John Stinson Farmer, Saxby opened a railway signalling works in Canterbury Road, around 1862. At its peak, the firm employed 2,000 people. All production was transferred to Wiltshire in 1903 and in 1906, the Kilburn site was sold. The photograph above was probably taken soon after, when part of the factory, including the large chimney, was demolished. Pictured below in 2001, the remaining building is used by a Housing Association.

In 1903, Lane and Son began working from No. 30 Netherwood Street, (since redeveloped as part of the Webheath Estate). Just two years later their main business was selling rather than moving furniture. They had left Netherwood Street by 1915. In the days before motorized lorries, Lane's No. 9 container is being pulled by a Burrell steam traction engine.

The façade of Kilburn Brewery, between Nos 293-313 Kilburn High Road, in 2001. In 1832 the brothers, George and William Verey, built a brewery on Kilburn High Road. Sold to Mitchell and Phillips in 1866, a fire almost destroyed the building in 1892, but it was rebuilt and extended. When the brewery finally closed in 1920 it employed sixty-six men.

Fredrick Handley Page pictured here in the early 1950s, founded his aircraft company in 1909. Three years later the firm moved from Barking to Cricklewood Lane, within easy reach of Hendon Aerodrome. Perhaps Frederick Handley Page's greatest contribution to aircraft design was the invention of the slotted wing, in 1919. Still in evidence today, it was designed to combat stalled flight which killed so many early aviators on take off and landing. Handley Page was also one of the first people to recognise the huge potential for civilian travel and he started one of the earliest commercial air services in 1919. He was knighted in 1942 and died in 1962.

In order to meet rising demand for aircraft in the First World War, Handley Page built a factory fronting Somerton and Claremont Roads. At the same time, 160 acres of adjacent land were compulsorily purchased for the site of Cricklewood Aerodrome. Handley Page also used the nearby Welsh Harp reservoir to test seaplanes. This aerial view looks west across the aerodrome in 1918; Edgware Road and the Midland Railway (now Thameslink) cross the photograph from left to right. There are several biplanes on the ground. In 1929 Handley Page moved to a new airfield at Radlett. They tried to get all planes away from Cricklewood before a fence was built that cut the factory off from the aerodrome. Unfortunately one remained, and could only take off after ramps were built to carry it over the new owner's fence! The factory finally closed in 1964-1965 and the site became a trading estate. Following a fire in 1984, one of the worst in London's recent history, the remaining buildings were progressively demolished and the site redeveloped as a housing estate.

*A 4-Engine Handley Page Aeroplane.*

The first V/1500 aircraft was assembled at Cricklewood in 1918. It was nicknamed the 'Super Handley' because of its size - there are thirty-four men standing under the 126ft wingspan. The prototype had a short life, crashing on a routine test flight in June 1918 over Golders Green, near Garrick Avenue. Five men died and there was just one survivor.

*2-Engine Handley Page — wings folded for housing.*

The 0/400 bomber was designed as 'a bloody paralyser of an aeroplane to stop the Hun in his tracks'. The wings could fold back to fit conventional hangars. In 1920, an 0/400 adapted for civil flight crashed near Cricklewood, in the back garden of No. 6 Basing Hill. Four died but there were four survivors, one of whom went missing. Regaining consciousness after the crash, Eric Studd could only remember he had to go to Paris. So he made his way to Victoria and caught the boat train!

At the end of the First World War, production at Cricklewood slumped. The work force was cut from 5,000 to just 100. Part of the new factory was rented out. In 1918 this hangar had been full of bombers; two years later the only plane was a 0/400, converted to carry civilians.

The Heyford was the last Handley Page biplane bomber ordered by the RAF. Its maiden flight was in 1930 but the Heyford never saw active service. Instead, it was more famous for looping the loop at the 1935 Hendon Airshow and for being the first aircraft to be detected on radar during demonstrations that same year.

The Cricklewood factory attracted a number of royal visitors. Here Queen Alexandra and Princess Victoria, accompanied by Frederick Handley Page, are being shown a bomber production line in March 1918. Apparently they were surprised at the large number of women employees and the variety of work they did.

Heracles was the world's first four-engine airliner, carrying just 38 passengers. During the 1930s Heracles was based at Croydon airport and by 1937, had clocked up a million miles in the air! On the London to Paris route, it carried more than 100,000 passengers in over 13,000 flying hours. Heracles was wrecked in a gale at Whitchurch in 1940.

In 1929 Cricklewood Aerodrome was sold to the Golders Green Development Corporation for over £100,000, and Handley Page moved to Radlett. Laings developed the estate with its distinctive oval road pattern centred on Pennine Drive, shown here soon after completion. The most famous inhabitant was the beautiful actress Jean Simmons who lived with her family at No.120 Cheviot Gardens in the 1930s. In a long career she starred in over fifty British and Hollywood films, and today lives in California.

In 1915, British Caudron established their works at No. 255 Cricklewood Broadway, later expanding to Nos 277-289. This plane was made by the French company, based at Rue near Le Touquet. British Caudron became a major supplier of components to Handley Page and employed 400 workers in 1919. The factory closed after the war ended and the site was later taken over by Rolls Razor.

Frank Smith was shown a French dish of thinly sliced potatoes cooked in oil and decided to sell his own version. In 1920 'Smith's Potato Crisps' began in two garages behind the Crown Public House. Demand grew rapidly, so in 1921, Smith moved into a disused part of the Handley Page factory in Somerton Road and also opened factories in Birmingham and Portsmouth. The following year the famous blue packet of salt was added. In 1938 Smith's moved from Cricklewood to a new factory on the North Circular Road.

The car above is one of the Bentleys that won the 24-hour Le Mans in 1929. Walter Owen Bentley or 'W.O.' as he was always known, founded Bentley Motors. Between 1919 and 1931, the Cricklewood Works in Oxgate Lane produced some of the world's most famous cars. The car below is a stripped down version of the 4.5 litre Blower Bentley converted to a single seater. In 1931, it set the outer circuit record at Brooklands at 137.6 mph. During the Second World War, Handley Page made unconventional use of several Bentleys, as barriers on their Radlett airfield, to prevent glider attacks.

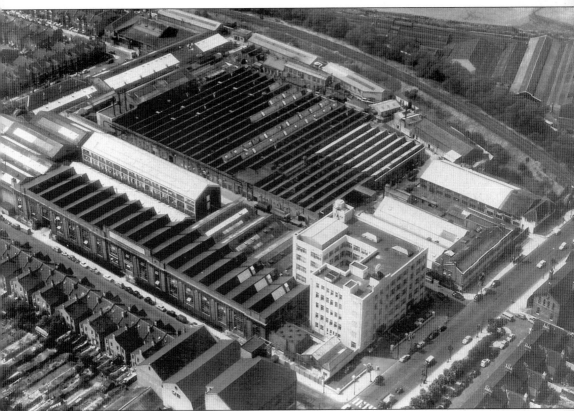

An aerial view of Smith's Industries on Edgware Road at Cricklewood, between Temple Road and the railway. Smiths' began as a family clock business in 1851. They went on to make mileometers for the expanding motor industry. Alan Gordon Smith invented and produced the first British speedometer, fitted to King Edward VII's car in 1904. In response to rising demand during the First World War, Smith's built a factory at Cricklewood in 1915. A year later they were employing 2,000 people, making millions of shell fuses, wire rope, spark plugs and aircraft instruments. After the war, motor accessories dominated production and huge numbers of clocks were also manufactured. During the Second World War, the workforce increased to 8,000. The Cricklewood factory was bombed in August 1940, but rapidly reconstructed. Foreign competition hit clock and watch production in the 1970s. At the same time, the decline in the UK motor industry adversely affected sales of motor accessories. The factory was demolished in 1985 and the site is currently occupied by a large DIY suppliers and discount clothing store.

The railway bridge across Edgware Road in 1937. An article that year suggested that Cricklewood should be renamed 'Clocklewood' reflecting the importance of Smith's as a major local employer.

Smith's Industries, Edgware Road. In 1921, the company headquarters moved here from Great Portland Street. Note the imposing electric clock on top of the building, a highly visible symbol of Smith's dominance. The headquarters moved to Childs Hill in the 1980s, and the company successfully diversified into aerospace and medical instrumentation. After several mergers, Smith's was renamed The Smith's Group PLC in 2000.

HRH Prince Philip visiting Smith's Industries at Cricklewood, on a rainy November day in 1959.

A mobile advertisement for Smith's Clocks appears on this company van, photographed in 1934.

The skyscraper pictured here is part of a proposed regeneration scheme for a 54 hectare site between the North Circular and Cricklewood Lane. In June 2001, Railtrack, in conjunction with Pillar Property, formed a joint venture company, Cricklewood Redevelopment Ltd. If the plans go ahead, 18,000 jobs will be created. It includes offices, housing and retail space, plus a new station on the Thameslink line.